Beg

Megan McGee

BookLeaf
Publishing

India | USA | UK

Presentation by *BookLeaf Publishing*

Web: www.bookleafpub.com

E-mail: info@bookleafpub.com

ISBN: 9789357696241

First edition 2023

DEDICATION

This book is for the heartbroken, whether it was yesterday or a lifetime ago, this is for you. Because you're not alone, I'm right here with you.

ACKNOWLEDGEMENT

Writing these poems and putting together this collection made it very obvious that I have so many beautiful people in my life. Thank you Mom for listening to the endless banter about this relationship and the last and encouraging me to be myself and write this book. Thank you to my friends, both those I've known for several years and just a few hours, Emily, Madeline, Alex, and Caleb for sitting around a dining table while the pizza got cold so I could read this collection and put them in the perfect order. You guys are amazing. And thank you Louis for listening to a bunch of poems, some about you and some about someone else, not knowing with full certainty which ones are which. You are also amazing and I love you.

PREFACE

When we think of heartbreak, we think of moments when we're alone after a breakup. Maybe there is a big fight, ending with broken glass and hurt feelings. Or maybe there isn't. Maybe the most gut-wrenching, isolating thing is when you realize your relationship is beginning to end. That's when you're a leper in your own home, when you're your own worst enemy and only ally. When there's something wrong and you don't know if it's you or if it's them, but you don't want it to be the relationship because then you'll be alone, like actually alone. So you fight it and you fight them and then you are left broken. That's where our journey begins.

Genesis

In the beginning,
There was a Word,
And the Word was Love,
And the Love was eternal,
But the person was not.

Cages

I

Boy was she magnificent.
Soaring through the sky,
She was weightless,
And she was strong.
And now she is mine

Her beauty was insurmountable,
Untouchable.
She was wild
As she called to me
Beckoning me to her world
But I was just a visitor in it.

I knew I must have her.

My gold cage compliments
the crimson of her feathers.
It suits her.

I will train her
to love her cage
as I love her.

She will appreciate her sanctuary
eventually.

I can change her mind.
Smooth those wild edges
Clip those wings
So she no longer needs to face the dangers
of the outside world

We will make a lovely pair
She and I.
I did enjoy her singing
and the way her feathers glistened in the sun.

Although
something has changed within her.
Now that she is mine.
She no longer sings.
She screams.

The crimson of her feathers is replaced
by the crimson of her blood as she

...pluck pluck plucks

I watch as she tears herself apart.
Weaving herself amongst the bars
Building and destroying

Now she is naked
Vulnerable
Now she needs me

But she is becoming less and less the bird I so
admired.
Without her feathers, she can no longer fly,
take over the sky.
She is no longer mine.

I open the cage to release the naked,
broken thing
But she has trapped herself
in a cage of crimson feathers.

Cages

I was once free to spread my wings,
To stretch
To feel the support of nothingness beneath me,
Now I sit,
With nothing to do but ponder

The nothingness was a comfort,
The breeze played with my eyelashes,
Caressed my cheek.
I itch to fatigue my breasts once more
To fight to stay afloat,
To defy gravity.

Now the wind taunts me.
Ruthless.
Mocking.
A reminder of what I once had.

And now I am his
I am safe from those who hunted me
So he says

No

I peer out of my enclosure,
Glancing at the face pressing closer
Once a friend
Now a captor.

I cannot take it.
A wild thing tamed
Broken

I pluck and weave myself amongst the bars.
I wish to hide.
I crave blindness.
I crave comfort.

...pluck pluck pluck

Where the breeze once tickled my whiskers,
It now cuts into flesh.
Raw flesh.

I must pluck and weave and nest.
Pluck, and weave, and nest.
Pluck weave nest

The face watches with muted concern.

Soon I will be in a cloud of familiar crimson
But at what cost?

I am naked.
There is no need for feathers
When you cannot fly.

Fully encapsulated in my own,
Blind to the outside.
No bating breezes.
No wicked winds.
Utter comfort.
Empty despair.
A new nothingness is a new home.
In a cage of crimson feathers.

Paper Dolls

I am a paper doll
As you dress me up in your ideal.
Lay paper dresses on me
But the tabs begin to peel

You trap me in their folds
Say you're looking for a trophy wife
With heavy expectations
But that will never be my life.

For a while I enjoy playing dress up
And I tell you that's all it is.
Because the dresses are pretty
But nothing you desire seems to fit

I have my tea length skirts
My mouth printed in a permanent grin
Accessories included
A sweeper mop and some children

You have your suits and your freedom
To speak as you please
You wear your emotions on your sleeve,
Because you're allowed to be angry

Soon I shed the disguise
Release the pressure you placed on me
Express my every desire
To also be that free

But no
I cannot
I am but a paper doll who is ripping at the
seems
I must never leave this house
You are protecting me, can't I see?

But the paper prison you put me in
Is much more fragile than me.

The Secret to Anti-Aging

Let me tell you a secret
To keep your face from wrinkling.
To keep your youth.
Don't frown.
Don't cry.
Don't smile.
Don't laugh.
Don't make silly faces when you're telling a story.
Don't show disappointment.
Don't care.

Just don't.
Because then you'll look older
Wiser
And we can't have that.
You must keep your infantilizing baby face
So that men can feel more manly
And everyone else can remain
Inferior.

Dear Me

Dear Me,
Nobody else is listening right now,
So you're it, babe.
I have some thoughts,
But none I can share
With anyone else
For fear they won't care.
Or they'll sharpen those words
And hold them to their throat
Asking, "is this what you want?"
Then point them to me, "Or is this?"
He'll jab them into me
In a fight that started
When I asked him to be present
As I show him my hurt feelings
Born from something he said.
Then he turns the tables
Round and round
To show me my mistakes.
And then I said I was sorry.
Have you come this far?
To try and please so many people,
But never who you are?
You let people walk all over you
In the name of nurturing their broken hearts

Isn't ours just as broken?
Don't we deserve care too?
To be listened to?
To be validated?
Just to be.
To be,
Or not to be,
That is the question.
To be broken,
To be sad,
To be happy,
Or to be mad,
Or,
To be nothing at all?
Can I let it all go?
This wretched feeling
That tears me apart.
Should I let it all go?

Yes and no.

Fantasy

i am not here to serve as your fantasy
i am broken
i am scarred
i am sure
i am strong
i am emotion
i am logic
i am so much more than a fantasy
i am woman
i am mine and no one else's

Today

Today I
- [ ] Kissed you on your way out the door
- [ ] Went to the gym
- [ ] Poured my heart into a scholarship essay
- [ ] Prayed that I get it so we don't have to start our lives together in debt
- [ ] Composed an application to my dream school to study for my dream career
- [ ] Cried about my broken foundation
- [ ] Wished I could talk to you about it
- [ ] Took a nap to recover from the emotional fatigue
- [ ] Decided to write a book
- [ ] Revised my essay
- [ ] Hit submit
- [ ] Avoided calls from my dad
- [ ] Cried about my fractured family
- [ ] Mourned the loss of trust
- [ ] Found myself pinned to the couch by the weight of it all
- [ ] Wished I could talk to you about it
- [ ] Peeled myself up to eat something

- ☐ Took a walk
- ☐ Felt lighter
- ☐ Wrote you a love letter
- ☐ Stuck it in your notebook
- ☐ You've been struggling too
- ☐ Was not okay
- ☐ Came to terms with that being okay
- ☐ Tended to my emotional wounds

What you noticed when you walked through the door

- ☐ I didn't clean the dishes from the night before

Celebrate

I would rather have no one to celebrate with
Than nothing to celebrate.

Whiskey Band-Aid

To be, or not to be
To drown or not to drown
Sometimes not to drown is not an option.
So the question can only be
To drown or to drown deeper?
To drown in an abyss of emotion
Or to slap a band-aid on the heartbreak and drown in
whisky instead?
Feel the heartbreak that pierces the mind
The body
And the soul;
Where there are no survivors

Or:

Subdue the beast and simply get to the next day?
A day away from the mallet that shattered
everything.
A day away from the knife in the back
A day further from the all-consuming acid trap that
is pain
That eats at your insides until you are nothing more
than the alcohol you consume
Poison in large quantities
But in small quantities?
In small quantities it can bring sleep to the sleepless
It can quiet the intrusive thoughts
Eventually it could destroy me
But for now, it's my whiskey Band-aid

Time

I

I wish I could stop time
So that I could take all the time
In the world getting over you
And not feel like my ovaries are shriveled
Or that I'm wasting the best years of my life
On a man
Who wasn't man enough to love me

Wolf in Sheep's Clothing

I wish you liked successful women
Because I will be successful
And I wish you wanted companionship
Because that's what I need
But you don't
You want a wife
The picket fence
Your love is currency
Paying for my masks
Your love is a disguise
A sheep in wolf's clothing
Pretending to be strong
Or unconditional
Or equal
It isn't equal at all
Because you wish I were a live-in maid
A nanny
Your mother but 26 years younger
But I flashed my teeth
And the mask dissolved
And you got scared
I am the wolf you tried to put in sheep's
clothing
So you could feel more like an alpha.

Rolling Stone

I am a rolling stone
Holding onto ties
That no longer serve me.

I am free
But I can't help but think
How life would have been
Had I let moss grow on me.

Instead I gather:
Nicks, cuts, bumps, and bruises,
Chips, splits, and jagged edges.

When carelessly handled,
I've been known to make others bleed.
And you have handled me carelessly.

From the beginning
I told you what I am,
With words, with actions,
with emotions, with love.

Because I loved what I am,
and that's good because I am what I am.
But you made it known that that was wrong.

Because I wasn't a quartz
or a pearl
or a mossy stone
ready to make a home.

Instead I am irregular,
unpredictable,
I don't look the same from any angle
So be careful.

And despite this warning,
You will blame me.
When it was you who picked up a rolling stone.
When you wanted something else entirely.

Now you toss me away,
And lick your wounds,
Expecting me to do the same
But I warned you.

I am a rolling stone
And now I am free to go back to loving me

Rose

A rosebush without any roses
is still a rosebush.
The fact that it hasn't bloomed
Has nothing to do with you.

April 5th

The moment I realized
Was just another Tuesday
On the 5th of April
Not an anniversary
But a dusty old date
Common
Mundane
But the feeling was all consuming
Like a fire of the soul
When I realized I don't love something with my
entire person
With every fiber of my being
Every hair on my head does not yet love every hair
on another's
And the pain was unexpected
It was not of the lack of love because the love is
within in me
Waiting

Kennedy

I'm hooked on you like smoke
Around a campfire in early fall
The high is a feeling of home
Being wrapped up in a red scarf
Made with love
With no downer
No hangover
Just warmth kissing your cheek
And the cold nipping at your nose
Fire and ice
Tangled in an everlasting dance
Filled with laughter and joy

Love

I love how you say the word love.

Like,
When you tell me you love
when I lay on your chest,
As you gently stroke your fingers through my hair.
They tell me secrets when they brush my ears.
And,
I love how you say the word love,
Just to see how it tastes on your lips,
How it feels on your breath.

Oh, how it feels in my heart!

I see you weighing the word,
Just four letters,
Just for me,
And for you?
Come,
Let's see if it suits us,
The way you suit me.

Because I love saying the word love too.

Love: The Conditioned Response

I have played this game before.
When the heart starts to flutter
And I make a fool of myself trying to chase it
To chase you.
In the beginning,
I shove that feeling down
To the deepest depths of my heart
Where I keep my secrets, fears, and desires
I keep it there until I know you won't laugh, leave,
or treat me poorly
Then you flash a trusting smile
Share some of your own secrets, fears, and desires.
And I do not laugh, leave, or treat you poorly
Instead
You spoil me and I spoil you
But I've played this game before
Lived this dream that soured and spoiled and turned
into a nightmare
Soon you will realize that you can do better than me
Your gifts will turn to currency
As his did
And we will fight and you will leave
Call me ugly
Call me needy
For now you say you love me.
But I have played this game before.

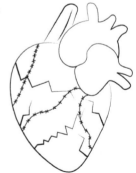

26

A Broken Mug

I am broken
Like a mug with a crack at the bottom
That's no good for coffee or tea
Or whiskey or bourbon.
Because it is damaged goods.

I'm afraid if you give me love
If you fill my cup
Give me an ounce
Or just a drop
It will leak from my veins
It will pool at my feet
Create a ring around my base
And stain your bedside table.

But I will be hooked
Utterly addicted
Searching for more and more
Until your cup is empty
And you have nothing left to give.

But what if I weren't a mug?
Not anymore.
What if now I can be something different
With you?
Like a vase.

Where I can take what I need
To nourish our relationship
And let the rest flow free
To be released to the world
And to be shared with others
Because love is not finite.

Meanwhile, I'll be
Somewhere to house a growing relationship,
A budding love.
One where we can grow together.

Where the Wind Blows

You say that I am your rock,
But I shift as sand does on the edge of a dune.
Just know that when you say I ground you,
You are a balloon strung to a kite.
Harmonious and oblivious we dance through the
night.
We spiral, we soar
Through tumultuous storms
But to you, I remain tethered.
And how could we be lost when we are together?

Time

II

I wish I could stop time
So that I could take all the time
In the world loving you
Soaking in your affection
Bathing you in mine
And stay here forever
You and me.